W9-APF-964

Eager Street Academy #884
401 East Eager Street
Baltimore, MD 21202

COMMUNITY · CONNECTIONS

HOW DO THEY HELP?
THE NATURE CONSERVANCY

BY KATIE MARSICO

Published in the United States of America by Cherry Lake Publishing
Ann Arbor, Michigan
www.cherrylakepublishing.com

Content Adviser: Rob Fischer, Ph.D., Professor and Director, Master of Nonprofit
Organizations, Jack, Joseph, and Morton Mandel School of Applied Social Sciences,
Case Western Reserve University
Reading Adviser: Marla Conn MS, Ed., Literacy specialist, Read-Ability, Inc.

Photo Credits: © Alf Ribeiro / Shutterstock.com, cover, 1, 5; © Vlad Teodor/Shutterstock, 7;
© Jerry and Marcy Monkman/EcoPhotography.com / Alamy Stock Photo, 9;
© WOLF AVNI/Shutterstock, 11; © Jimmyostgard | Dreamstime.com, 13;
© DavorLovincic/istock, 15; © Jerry Monkman/Nature Picture Library/Corbis, 17;
© Andrezej Kubik/Shutterstock, 19; © omgimages/Thinkstock, 21

LIBRARY OF CONGRESS CATALOGING-IN-PUBLICATION DATA
Names: Marsico, Katie, 1980- author.
Title: The Nature Conservancy / by Katie Marsico.
Other titles: Community connections (Cherry Lake Publishing)
Description: Ann Arbor, Michigan : Cherry Lake Publishing, [2016] |
Series: Community connections: how do they help? | Audience: K to grade 3. |
    Includes bibliographical references and index.
Identifiers: LCCN 2015048732| ISBN 9781634710510 (hardcover) |
    ISBN 9781634712491 (pbk.) | ISBN 9781634711500 (pdf) |
    ISBN 9781634713481 (ebook)
Subjects: LCSH: Nature Conservancy (U.S.)–History–Juvenile literature. |
    Nature conservation–History–Juvenile literature. | Endangered
    ecosystems–Juvenile literature.
Classification: LCC QH76 .M37 2016 | DDC 333.72/0601—dc23
LC record available at https://lccn.loc.gov/2015048732

Cherry Lake Publishing would like to acknowledge the
work of The Partnership for 21st Century Learning. Please
visit www.p21.org for more information.

Printed in the United States of America
Corporate Graphics Inc.
CLFA11

THE NATURE CONSERVANCY

CONTENTS

HOW DO THEY HELP?

SAVING NATURAL SETTINGS

The Atlantic Forest of Brazil is home to tens of thousands of plants and animals. Yet **deforestation** and other human activities have threatened their survival.

That is why the Nature Conservancy is taking steps to replant 1 billion trees in this tropical rain forest. It is committed to protecting Earth's land and water for both people and wildlife.

The Nature Conservancy knows that replanting trees is just one step in the journey to protect the environment.

Think about how planting trees is good for the environment. For starters, trees provide shelter and shade for wildlife. They also remove carbon dioxide from the air during **photosynthesis**. Since carbon dioxide creates pollution, trees help keep the environment clean.

5

The Nature Conservancy is one of the world's leading **conservation** groups. Its efforts span more than 35 countries, including the United States and Canada. Nature Conservancy scientists are constantly trying to find new and better ways of protecting the environment and **biodiversity**. This organization works to restore, or save, the natural settings that both humans and wildlife depend on to survive.

Trees and plants are at risk from threats both natural (like disease) and human-created (like deforestation).

Are you able to guess how much land the Nature Conservancy has helped save? (Hint: Guess big!) So far, this organization has conserved 120 million acres (49 million hectares). That's an area larger than the state of California!

THE PAST AND PRESENT

In 1946, a group of U.S. scientists teamed up to form the **Ecologists** Union. Their goal was to save natural settings that were threatened by human activities. By 1950, members of the Ecologists Union had renamed their group the Nature Conservancy. The following year, the Nature Conservancy was officially recognized as a **nonprofit** organization in Washington, D.C.

Many people enjoy exploring nature. The Nature Conservancy helps protect natural places.

Think about what a nonprofit organization does. In business, a profit represents the difference between an amount gained and an amount spent. Businesses try and make as much profit as they can. Yet nonprofit groups such as the Nature Conservancy are focused on supporting a specific cause rather than earning profit.

During the next few years, the Nature Conservancy began purchasing wilderness areas that it hoped to protect. In others cases, it convinced landowners to either sell or donate specific rights to their property so the land could be better protected. For example, the Nature Conservancy persuaded certain ranchers and farmers to limit their development of the land. It also encouraged such individuals to be more careful about their use of **natural resources**.

Large farms can be a problem for the environment. They need lots of flat, open space.

The Nature Conservancy's main offices are located in Arlington, Virginia. So how does the group work with foreign governments to carry out its conservation efforts around the world? Look online or contact the Nature Conservancy directly to find out.

11

The Nature Conservancy started carrying out controlled fires called prescribed burns. Fires are a natural part of how ecosystems renew themselves. A prescribed burn involves setting fire to a natural area in a controlled way in hopes of clearing out **invasive** plants. Such plants often threaten the survival of native wildlife. Prescribed burns therefore help restore forests and grasslands to their original state.

Controlled burns look dangerous but they're an important part of the Nature Conservancy's work.

LOOK!

Head to the library or go online to look for images of the Nature Conservancy conducting prescribed burns. What do you notice about these photographs? How do they seem different than pictures of uncontrolled wildfires?

13

Today, the Nature Conservancy continues to use a variety of methods to protect Earth's land and water. To succeed, it relies on both volunteers and paid staff, including roughly 600 scientists. These men and women study the best ways to balance the needs of people and nature. The Nature Conservancy also depends on several other types of workers, including legal and financial experts, educators, and firefighters.

14

Some Nature Conservancy staff spend their time outside, others work mostly in offices.

Are you able to guess who funds the Nature Conservancy? (Hint: There are a few correct answers to this question!) Some funding comes from membership dues and donations of money and land. The Nature Conservancy also receives government support.

ENCOURAGING CONSERVATION

The Nature Conservancy accomplishes its mission in many different ways. Planting trees, working with landowners, and organizing prescribed burns are just a few. They also partner with businesses ranging from airlines to department stores. Thanks to the Nature Conservancy, these companies learn how to become more

The better Nature Conservancy workers understand the environment, the better they can protect it.

16

Which companies is the Nature Conservancy currently partnered with? How are such businesses helping save Earth's land and water? Contact the Nature Conservancy or search online to answer these and other questions.

17

environmentally friendly and limit their use of natural resources.

The Nature Conservancy teams up with government agencies, too. Together, they ensure that natural areas are being properly cared for. Several **indigenous** communities also have a strong relationship with the Nature Conservancy. These communities depend on a healthy environment for their survival. For this reason, the Nature Conservancy raises awareness about environmental threats to indigenous peoples.

People who live in remote parts of the world rely more heavily on a healthy environment.

Look for books, magazines, and online articles that provide information about indigenous communities. Try to find photographs that demonstrate how indigenous peoples rely on nature. How do you think problems such as pollution and deforestation affect their lives?

19

One of the Nature Conservancy's largest efforts involves teaching the public the importance of respecting the environment. It publishes a magazine that reinforces this message. The group also organizes educational programming.

The Nature Conservancy helps people learn why land and water shouldn't be taken for granted. It is dedicated to protecting the natural world and its biodiversity.

When you enjoy and care for nature, you're helping the Nature Conservancy do its job!

Ready to support the Nature Conservancy? Use paper, crayons, and markers to create a map of your community. Label rivers, forest preserves, and any other natural areas that feature biodiversity. Afterward, talk to friends and family about local conservation efforts.

GLOSSARY

biodiversity (bye-oh-duh-VUHR-suh-tee) the existence of many kinds of plants and animals in a certain environment

conservation (kan-suhr-VAY-shuhn) the act of protecting the environment and the plants and animals that live in it

deforestation (dee-for-uh-STAY-shuhn) the act of burning or cutting down all the trees in a certain area

ecologists (ee-KAH-luh-jists) scientists who study the groups of living things and their environments

indigenous (in-DIH-juh-nuhs) living or existing naturally in a particular region or environment

invasive (in-VAY-siv) types of species that, once introduced into an environment, spread throughout it and harm native plants and animals

natural resources (NA-chuh-ruhl REE-sors-uhz) materials or substances that occur in nature

nonprofit (nahn-PRAH-fit) not existing for the main purpose of earning more money than is spent

photosynthesis (foh-toh-SIN-thi-sis) the process by which a green plant uses light to turn water and carbon dioxide into food

FIND OUT MORE

BOOKS

Claus, Matteson. *Animals and Deforestation*. New York: Gareth Stevens Publishing, 2014.

Hawley, Ella. *Exploring Our Impact on the Environment*. New York: PowerKids Press, 2013.

Owen, Ruth. *Zoologists and Ecologists*. New York: PowerKids Press, 2014.

WEB SITES

Earth Rangers—The Kids' Conservation Organization
www.earthrangers.org/our-programs/
Head here to learn more about simple, everyday activities that have a positive impact on the environment.

National Aeronautics and Space Administration (NASA)—Climate Kids
climatekids.nasa.gov/how-to-help/
Check out this site for information on different ways to support conservation, including planting a tree!

23

INDEX

ABOUT THE AUTHOR

Katie Marsico is the author of more than 200 children's books. She lives in a suburb of Chicago, Illinois, with her husband and children.

24